THE

# *DAILY SPARK*

*180 easy-to-use lessons and class activities!*

# THE DAILY SPARK

Critical Thinking
Journal Writing
Poetry
Pre-Algebra
SAT: English Test Prep
Shakespeare
Spelling & Grammar
U.S. History
Vocabulary
Writing

THE
# *DAILY SPARK*
# *U.S. History*

SPARKNOTES is a registered trademark of SparkNotes LLC

This edition published by Spark Publishing.

Spark Publishing
A Division of SparkNotes LLC
120 Fifth Avenue, 8th Floor
New York, NY 10011

ISBN 1-4114-0226-X

Please submit comments or report errors to *www.sparknotes.com/errors*.

Written by Nathan Barber.

Printed and bound in the United States.

*A Barnes & Noble Publication*

# Introduction

The Daily Spark series gives teachers an easy way to transform downtime into productive time. The 180 exercises—one for each day of the school year—will take students five to ten minutes to complete and can be used at the beginning of class, in the few moments before turning to a new subject, or at the end of class.

The exercises in this book may be photocopied and handed out to the class, projected as a transparency, or even read aloud. In addition to class time use, they can be assigned as homework exercises or extra credit problems.

The *U.S. History Daily Spark* teaches students about the most important events in our nation's history, from colonial times to the present day. Each exercise encourages critical thinking and creativity. Whether students are writing a first-person diary entry about the first harsh winter in the colonies, analyzing the phrase "the shot heard 'round the world," or thinking about how the terrorist attacks of September 11 changed their community, they will be engaged with and interested by history.

Spark your students' interest with the *U.S. History Daily Spark*!

# "Discovering" America

Christopher Columbus is often credited with "discovering" America, although the land he discovered was already inhabited. Imagine that you are one of the Native Americans who was living in North America when Columbus arrived. You later learn that he has taken credit for the "discovery" of your home. Write a response to his claim.

Christopher Columbus "discovered" America in October 1492.

# God, Gold, and Glory

During the Age of Discovery, European adventurers explored North America. Some historians say that these men were motivated by God, gold, and glory. What do you think historians mean by this?

The "Age of Discovery" was the period of exploration beginning in the mid-fifteenth century and ending in the mid-seventeenth century.

# Trader on the Coast

Imagine that you are a trader aboard a ship that is traveling the Triangle Trade route. Create a journal entry that describes a stop along the African coast. Include details about the goods you traded there and the people with whom you traded.

**The trade pattern known as the Triangle Trade route was developed in the 1500s.**

# Forced to Eat Dogs

The first permanent English settlement in North America was Jamestown, Virginia. The conditions were bad: settlers clashed with Native Americans and, once the food ran out, were forced to eat rats, mice, dogs, and cats. Imagine you are a settler dealing with these troubles. Write a letter to your family back in England describing your situation.

**Jamestown, Virginia was settled in 1607.**

# Native American

Who was Squanto, and what is he remembered for?

**Squanto died in 1622.**

# A War Against the Native Americans

During the Pequot War, American settlers burned a Native American village. The fire killed hundreds of Native Americans, including women and children. Imagine you are a survivor of this fire who lives in the devastated village. Write an account of what happened.

**The Pequot War occurred in 1637.**

# Not One Community, but Many

Some of the first colonies in North America were founded by people looking for a place to practice their religion freely. But instead of creating one large community open to all faiths, the first settlers created a number of different religious communities. Why do you think this happened?

**The first colonies included Providence (est. 1636), founded by Roger Williams; the Massachusetts Bay Colony (est. 1630), settled by the Massachusetts Bay Company and John Winthrop; and Pennsylvania (est. 1681), settled by Sir William Penn.**

# A Few Trinkets

In a remarkable transaction, the Dutch West India Company bought what is now Manhattan—all 22,000 acres of it—from the Native Americans living there for a few trinkets worth about $24. Imagine that you are a journalist present during the transaction, and write a short article about it.

The Dutch East India Company was established in 1606.  Peter Minuit bought Manhattan from the Native Americans in 1626.

# Fire and Brimstone

A religious revival called the Great Awakening swept across the colonies in the 1730s and 1740s, taking the colonists by storm. With their "hellfire and brimstone" sermons, preachers ignited scores of followers, some of whom tried to convert the Native Americans and the slaves. A divide separated the older, more traditional clergy and the people who participated in the Great Awakening. The traditionalists were taken aback by the new methods of preaching and by the passionate responses of the people who experienced revival. Why do you think the traditionalists reacted as they did?

The Great Awakening began in 1734 with the rousing teachings of the preacher Jonathan Edwards.

# The United States of France

When Britain controlled the colonies, France tried several times to take control of North America. Imagine what North America might be like today if France had succeeded. What would we eat, wear, do for fun? What would we believe?

**The British and the French fought over the land in the Americas between 1757 and 1763. The war is referred to either as the French and Indian War or as the Seven Years War.**

# Goods and Crops

According to the theory of mercantilism maintained by British colonialists before the American Revolution, colonies existed solely for the economic benefit of the mother country. Why would it be beneficial for Britain to permit the selling of colonial goods and crops in Britain only, and not in any other countries? Do you think restricting the sale of goods and crops was a win-win situation for both Britain and the colonies? Explain.

The term "mercantilism" was coined by economist Adam Smith in 1776.

# A Tax on Paper

In 1764 and 1765, Britain raised taxes in the colonies to beef up the British budget and to pay for an increased military presence in the colonies. The Stamp Act, for example, taxed all sorts of paper items, including legal documents, newspapers, pamphlets, marriage licenses, and even playing cards. Colonists didn't appreciate these taxes and insisted that only the colonial legislatures could raise the colonies' taxes. They argued that they should not suffer from British taxation without representation in British Parliament. Imagine you are one of these colonists. Write a letter to Parliament expressing your concern about the Stamp Act.

**The British Parliament passed the Stamp Act in 1765 and repealed it in 1766.**

# Defending Taxes

When North American colonists protested at the taxes Britain was levying, Parliament replied that the colonists were still British subjects under British law, so they were subject to British taxation. Parliament said that it represented all British subjects, even the colonists across the Atlantic Ocean, who didn't have representatives in Parliament. Using this information, imagine you are a member of the British Parliament and write a response to the colonists who are complaining about taxation without representation.

© 2004 SparkNotes LLC

**The colonists convened the Stamp Act Congress in 1765 to address the British Parliament's tax law.**

# Getting Tough with the Colonists

After such incidents as the Boston Tea Party and the decision by the Continental Congress to begin a complete boycott of British goods, the British government decided to get tough with the rebellious colonists. In your opinion, was there a "good guy" and a "bad guy" in this situation? If so, which was which, and why?

**The Boston Tea Party took place in 1775.**

# The Shot Heard Round the World

In April 1775, British troops, nicknamed **redcoats** because of their uniforms, descended on Lexington, Massachusetts, in an attempt to quell mounting opposition and to seize colonial guns and ammunition. They fired into a crowd, killing eight people. Ralph Waldo Emerson called the engagement in Lexington "the shot heard round the world." What do you think Emerson meant by this?

**Emerson was born in 1803 and died in 1882.**

# Hiding Behind Rocks

Britain's army was taught to fight in an orderly fashion, marching in straight lines and moving as a large group. The colonists, a more ragtag bunch, resorted to hiding behind trees and rocks and making sneak attacks on their opponents. Which method of fighting would you rather use if you were involved in a battle, and why?

**The Revolutionary War lasted from 1776 to 1783.**

# Revolution or Independence?

Some historians refer to the war between the American colonies and Britain as the American Revolution. Others say it should be known as the War for American Independence. Which do you favor? Write a paragraph or two explaining why you believe one name or the other is more appropriate.

The American Revolution (or the War for American Independence) began in 1776 and ended with the Treaty of Paris in 1783.

# Choosing Rebellion

On June 7, 1776, the Continental Congress met in Philadelphia. Members of the Congress spent nearly a month debating the best course of action for the Americans, and ultimately decided to declare themselves independent of British rule. What might have been some arguments in favor of remaining loyal to Britain? What might have been some arguments in favor of declaring independence?

**The Continental Congress settled on independence on July 2, 1776.**

# We're for Real

The Declaration of Independence didn't make the Americans independent of Britain—they had to fight a war to gain independence. And after the war was over, the Declaration of Independence didn't earn the United States automatic respect in the eyes of other nations. To become an official nation, the United States needed other countries to recognize it formally. What do you think were some of the obstacles the United States might have had to overcome in order to convince other countries that the new nation was for real?

**Members of the Continental Congress officially endorsed the Declaration of Independence on July 4, 1776.**

# Writing Down the Rules

The English constitution was not a written document—it was more informal. When the time came for the Americans to draft their own constitution, they decided they needed a written constitution. Why do you think a written constitution seemed like such a good idea?

**The American Constitution was drafted in 1787 and ratified by individual states in 1788.**

# Strong Government

Some founding fathers, called **Federalists**, favored a strong central government. Others, called **Anti-Federalists**, favored a weak one. Imagine you are a Federalist. What are some of your reasons for wanting a strong central government?

**Between 1787 and 1788, Alexander Hamilton, John Jay, and James Madison anonymously published a series of essays advocating a strong federal government. These essays are known as *The Federalist Papers*.**

# Weak Government

The first constitution that the United States adopted was known as the Articles of Confederation. The Articles created a very weak central government, especially compared with the monarchy of Britain. Considering the government under which most of the colonists had spent their lives, why do you think the writers of the Articles wanted such a weak central government?

**The Articles of Confederation were adopted in 1781.**

# Whiskey Rebellion

You've heard of people rebelling over oppression or unjust rulers, but whiskey? In 1794, a group of Pennsylvania farmers did just that, rebelling over the drink. What motivated them?

# Saving the People From an Autocrat

In 1926, Supreme Court Justice Louis Brandeis said of America's principle of separate branches of government (the judicial, legislative, and executive), "The purpose was, not to avoid friction, but, by means of the inevitable friction incident to the distribution of the governmental powers among three departments, to save the people from autocracy." What did Justice Brandeis mean by this? Translate his statement into simpler words. (Note that **autocracy** means government by one person.)

Louis Brandeis was born in 1856 and died in 1941.

# Power to the States

The framers of the Constitution decided that some powers should be held only by the federal government, and not be shared by the state governments. Some of these powers include coining money, conducting foreign affairs, declaring war, and fixing standard weights and measures. What kind of problems might have been created if, for example, states had the power to conduct foreign affairs? Imagine one such problem and write a paragraph about it.

The framers drafted the Constitution in the summer of 1787.

# We the People

A **preamble** is a statement of purpose. Below is the preamble to the U.S. Constitution, broken down into several lines. Rewrite each of the following lines in your own words.

We the people of the United States, in order to form a more perfect union,
establish justice,
insure domestic tranquility,
provide for the common defense,
promote the general welfare,
and secure the blessings of liberty to ourselves and our posterity,
do ordain and establish this Constitution for the United States of America.

The Constitution was drafted in the summer of 1787 and ratified by the states in 1788.

# Taking on the Creditors

Financial guru Alexander Hamilton believed that the new federal government should assume each state's burden of debt. Hamilton felt that the federal government, not the states, should deal with creditors. How do you think states with small debts might have reacted to the news that the federal government would assume even the largest of state debts?

**Alexander Hamilton served as America's first Secretary of the Treasury. With John Jay and James Madison, he wrote *The Federalist Papers*.**

# The First Five

Read the first five amendments of the Bill of Rights, listed below. Which amendments do you think are the most important for U.S. citizens? Why? Place the first five amendments in order of greatest importance to least importance, as you see it.

**Amendment I** Congress shall make no law respecting an establishment of religion, or prohibiting the free exercise thereof; or abridging the freedom of speech or of the press; or the right of the people peaceably to assemble and to petition the government for a redress of grievances.

**Amendment II** A well-regulated militia, being necessary to the security of a free state, the right of the people to keep and bear arms, shall not be infringed.

**Amendment III** No soldier shall in time of peace be quartered in any house without the consent of the owner, nor in time of war, but in a manner to be prescribed by law.

**Amendment IV** The right of the people to be secure in their persons, houses, papers, and effects, against unreasonable searches and seizures, shall not be violated, and no warrants shall issue but upon probable cause, supported by oath or affirmation and particularly describing the place to be searched and the persons or things to be seized.

**The Bill of Rights was adopted in 1791.**

# Speaking Freely

The First Amendment guarantees Americans freedom of speech, religion, and assembly, and the freedom to petition the government. How do you think your everyday life might change if you were not guaranteed freedom of speech?

© 2004 SparkNotes LLC

**The Bill of Rights was adopted in 1791.**

# We're Here and We're Hungry

Imagine that the Third Amendment (which forbids the forced quartering of troops in Americans' homes) did not exist, and that troops have just arrived in your living room, demanding food and a place to sleep. Write an email to a friend describing your reaction and feelings.

# Speedy and Public

The Sixth Amendment guarantees those accused of crimes a speedy and public trial as well as the right to call their own witnesses. Explain how a trial might be unfair without these provisions.

# The Veep

Under the Constitution, what are the vice president's duties?

# The Freedom to Accuse

In 1735, the governor of New York sued a German-born editor, John Peter Zenger, for seditious libel. The only problem was that the accusations that Zenger had made in his paper were true. Zenger was found not guilty, which marked an immense victory for freedom of the press.

Imagine that Zenger had been found guilty, and from then on newspapers weren't allowed to publish true accusations. What would some of the consequences be?

# Making the Compromise

The Great Compromise said that states' populations would determine their representation in the House of Representatives but would have no effect on their representation in the Senate—every state would get equal representation in the Senate. Why do you think both large and small states were comfortable with this arrangement?

**The Great Compromise was reached at the Constitutional Convention during the summer of 1797.**

# Create a Cabinet

As president, George Washington created a group of advisors called a **cabinet**. The first cabinet had three members: Secretary of State, Secretary of the Treasury, and Secretary of War. If you were president, what kind of cabinet would you have? Which three secretaries would you appoint first?

George Washington served as president from 1789 to 1797. His Secretary of State was Thomas Jefferson; his Secretary of the Treasury was Alexander Hamilton; his Secretary of War was General Henry Knox.

# Sticking to Two Terms

Many of George Washington's friends and supporters urged him to run for a third term as president, but President Washington decided against running. He believed it was important not to give one person too much time, and therefore power, in office. By refusing a third term and encouraging others to limit their terms to two, Washington created a precedent. Make a list of positive and negative consequences of limiting the presidential term.

**George Washington served as President of the United States from 1789 to 1797.**

# Fifty Times More Efficient

Eli Whitney invented a machine called the cotton gin that separated cotton from cotton seed. Using the machine was fifty times more efficient than separating the cotton and the seed by hand. What effects do you think the cotton gin had on the cotton business in the South?

© 2004 SparkNotes LLC

**Eli Whitney invented the cotton gin in 1793.**

# Making Slow Progress

John Adams once said,

"America is a great, unwieldy body. Its progress must be slow."

**What do you think Adams meant by this?** Describe a current event that proves his statement true or false.

**John Adams served as the second President of the United States from 1797 to 1801.**

# You Can't Say That

Under the Sedition Act (**sedition** means to stir up rebellion), a man named James Callender was fined and imprisoned for making the following statement about then-President John Adams:

> "He has never opened his lips, or lifted his pen, without threatening and scolding. The grand object of his administration has been to exasperate the rage of contending parties, to calumniate and destroy every man who differs from his opinions."

Would you approve or disapprove of a modern politician who tried to bring back the Sedition Act? What would you say to such a politician?

**Congress passed the Alien and Sedition Act in 1798.**

# The Court Puts Its Foot Down

For the first time in U.S. history, in the decision of *Marbury v. Madison*, the Supreme Court determined that an act of Congress was unconstitutional. What is the significance of the Supreme Court's ability to determine the constitutionality of an act of Congress or a law?

The *Marbury v. Madison* decision was handed down in 1803.

# Entangling Alliances

In his inaugural address, President Thomas Jefferson remarked,

> "Peace, commerce, and honest friendship, with all nations—entangling alliances with none."

What did Jefferson mean by "entangling alliances"? Do you believe this was a wise policy for such a young nation? Why or why not?

**Thomas Jefferson served as President from 1801 to 1809.**

# Slimming Down the Army

Thomas Jefferson believed that a large standing army (that is, a large permanent army) might lead to a dictator or a dictatorial government. As a result of his distrust of armies, he reduced the United States military to a paltry 2,500 men. Do you agree with Jefferson that a large army is risky? Why or why not?

Thomas Jefferson reduced the army in May 1801.

# You Are James Monroe

Imagine that you are James Monroe. Thomas Jefferson has sent you to Paris to purchase the port city of New Orleans from Napoleon for no more than $10 million. Write a letter to President Jefferson explaining that you went over budget, buying all 820,000 square miles of the Louisiana Territory from Napoleon for $15 million, or about three cents per acre. With this purchase, you have more than doubled the size of the American lands. Justify your actions.

**America bought the Louisiana Territory from France in 1803.**

# The First Occupation

Which foreign city was the first to be occupied by American forces? Under what circumstances was the city occupied?

# Making a Statement

When the United States defeated Britain in the War of 1812 (also known as the Second War of American Independence), the U.S. made a statement not only to Britain but also to the rest of the world. What do you think this statement was? Describe it in one or two sentences.

The War of 1812 took place between 1812 and 1815.

# Our Neighbor to the North

Canada and the United States may feel mild dislike for each other now, but feelings once ran stronger on both sides: the year America tried to conquer Canada, which was a colony of Britain at the time. America burned what is now Toronto, and British forces burned Washington, D.C. What effect do you think this war had on Canada–U.S. relations? Can you imagine the two countries clashing again? Explain your answers.

America attacked Canada in 1813.

# Spinning Yarn

The Boston Manufacturing Company employed mostly young women, who worked for a few years after leaving school and before getting married. Conditions for these women were often dangerous, and their private lives were closely controlled. Imagine you are one of these young workers and write a diary entry about your life.

The Boston Manufacturing Company was founded in 1814.

# Slave States, Free States

Under the Missouri Compromise, the U.S. admitted Missouri as a slave state and Maine as a free state. This compromise maintained a balance in the Union of free states and slave states. Why do you think both slave states and free states wanted an equal number of each kind of state in the Union?

**The Missouri Compromise was reached in 1820.**

# Memo to Europe:
# Mind Your Own Business

In 1823, President James Monroe, with the help of his advisors, developed what became known as the Monroe Doctrine. The Monroe Doctrine said that the United States would not allow any European nation to intervene in or colonize countries in the Western Hemisphere in any way at any time for any reason. Do you believe that Monroe had the right to tell other countries to stay out of the Western Hemisphere? Explain.

© 2004 SparkNotes LLC

James Monroe was President from 1817 to 1825.

# Bear Hunter

Andrew Jackson, famous for hunting bear and fighting "Indians," swept the South and the West during the presidential election of 1828. Why do you think the rugged Jackson had such appeal in these regions? Why do you think he didn't carry any state in the Northeast?

**Andrew Jackson, the nation's seventh president, served from 1829 to 1837.**

# Thanks for Your Help

After Andrew Jackson became president, he rewarded many of his supporters with high-level government jobs. This practice became known as the **spoils system**, and many of Jackson's critics objected to it, calling it unethical. What do you think? If you were president, would you give your friends plum jobs? Why or why not?

**Andrew Jackson served as president from 1829 to 1837.**

# To the Bad Lands

The U.S. government wanted to expand America's borders westward, but Native Americans inhabited that land. The government dealt with this by forcibly relocating many Native Americans to reservations on arid land far from their homes. Imagining that you are an advisor to President Andrew Jackson, create a proposal for westward expansion that is favorable to both the government and the Native American population.

Between 1816 and 1840, tribes located between the original states and the Mississippi River, including Cherokees, Chickasaws, Choctaws, Creeks, and Seminoles, were forced to sign more than forty treaties ceding their lands to the U.S.

# A Price on Your Head

Harriet Tubman, an ex-slave, was famous for helping over 300 people escape slavery via the Underground Railroad. Many people wanted her dead; at one point, the price on her head was $40,000. If you knew there was a huge price on your head, do you think you would continue to risk your life to help others, or would you simply try to keep yourself safe? Explain your answer.

Harriet Tubman was born around 1820 and died in 1913. The Underground Railroad is believed to have been established in 1787.

# One-Room Schoolhouse

Some of the earliest public schools in America were schoolhouses where eight grades were taught by one teacher in one room. How does your school differ from the first public schools in America?

**The Boston Latin School, America's first public school, was established in 1635.**

# The Infamous Painter

Who was the first person to attempt to assassinate a U.S. president? What happened?

**This assassination attempt took place in 1835.**

# Mary Lyon and Mount Holyoke

In 1837, Mary Lyon opened what is now Mount Holyoke College as an institution of higher learning for women. Almost from the start, there were more applicants than slots available. Many other such institutions experienced the same boom in applications. If you were a woman of college age in 1837, do you think you would have wanted to attend Mount Holyoke? Explain your answer.

**Mary Lyon was born in 1797 and died in 1849.**

# Studying the States

The Frenchman Alexis de Tocqueville spent ten months in America before writing his famous book, *Democracy in America*. If you were going to write a book about another country, how long would you want to spend in that country? What country would you choose? What kinds of things would you want to observe? Explain your answers.

**De Tocqueville published the first volume of *Democracy in America* in 1835 and the second volume in 1840.**

# Two Parties Have the Power

From the 1840s on, Americans have essentially employed a two-party system, meaning that only two political parties vie for power during major elections. Make a list of some of the advantages and disadvantages of having only two major parties in power.

The first two major political parties in the United States were the Federalists and the Anti-Federalists. Today, the two major political parties are the Democrats and the Republicans.

# The Nation of Texas

Texas won a precarious independence from Mexico in 1836, but Mexico wouldn't recognize Texas as an independent country. In an attempt to win recognition as a nation, Texas negotiated with Belgium, France, and Holland. But it turned out to be Britain that was most interested in Texas's bid to be recognized as a nation. Why do you think Britain wanted to see Texas become a full-fledged nation?

**Texas became the twenty-eighth state in 1845.**

# Westward Ho

**Manifest Destiny** is the idea that it was the United States' destiny to expand westward across the continent, all the way to the Pacific Ocean. Do you think westward expansion was truly the United States's destiny? Why or why not?

John O'Sullivan, editor of the *Democratic Review*, coined the phrase "Manifest Destiny" in an 1845 article.

# California: Rock-bound and Cheerless?

Daniel Webster is reported to have said of what is now California,

> "What do we want with this vast, worthless area? This region of savages and wild beasts, of deserts and shifting sands and whirlwinds of dust, of cactus and prairie dogs. . . . What can we ever hope to do with the western coast, a coast of three-thousand miles, rock-bound, cheerless, uninviting, and not a harbor on it?"

Write Webster a short letter about what California is like today.

California was admitted to the Union in 1850 as the thirtieth state.

# Heading West in a Wagon

Imagine that you and your family have loaded a wagon and are heading for unsettled land in the Oregon Territory. Write a journal entry about the things you have seen along the way and what you plan to do once you arrive in Oregon.

**Congress created the Oregon Territory in August 1848.**

# Striking It Rich

In 1848, miners discovered a precious substance in California: gold. Within a year, prospectors flocked to California determined to strike it rich. Write a letter to your family explaining that you have "gold fever" and are headed to California to make your fortune.

# A National Road

In 1852, the famed Cumberland Road, or National Road, was finally completed. It stretched from Maryland to Illinois, covering nearly 600 miles and five states. How do you think the towns along the highway benefited from the new traffic?

**The National Road is now part of U.S. Route 40.**

# Hinton Helper's Manuscript

Imagine that you are an editor at a major publishing company in 1857. You have just read a manuscript entitled *The Impending Crisis of the South* by Hinton Helper. Helper, a Southerner who hates both African-Americans and slavery, argues in his manuscript that non–slave owners in the South are badly off as a result of slavery. As an editor, how would you respond to Helper?

**Hinton Helper was born in 1829 and died in 1909.**

# I Dunno

Who were the **Know-Nothings**, and how did they get their name? If you're not sure, come up with an educated guess.

The Know-Nothings gained prominence during the 1850s.

# 1,000 Steamboats

By 1860, there were an estimated one thousand steamboats on the Mississippi River. How do you think river transportation, especially by steamboat, changed such things as travel, trade, communication, and military strategy?

**Engineer Robert Fulton patented his design for the first successful steamboat in 1809.**

# On the Railroad

Compile a list of ten reasons why railroad transportation was more desirable and potentially more profitable than river transportation.

The first railroad charter in North America was granted to John Stevens in 1815.

# Not-So-Famous

Take a look at the two lists below, and then answer the question that follows.

| **Famous Presidents** | **Not-So-Famous Presidents** |
| --- | --- |
| George Washington | Martin Van Buren |
| Thomas Jefferson | Millard Fillmore |
| Andrew Jackson | Franklin Pierce |
| Abraham Lincoln | James Buchanan |

Pick one of the famous presidents and explain why you think he is better known than one of the more obscure presidents.

# Free Soil

In 1846 in Missouri, a slave named Dred Scott sued his owner for his freedom in both state and federal court. Scott claimed that he had been living on free soil in Illinois and the Wisconsin Territory for more than five years and that in consequence, he was free. The Supreme Court ultimately decided that to make Scott free would be to deprive his owner of property. If the Supreme Court had granted Dred Scott his freedom, what would it have meant for slaves throughout the South?

**The Supreme Court ruled on the case in 1857.**

# Settling in the North

Although there were perhaps hundreds of thousands of European immigrants in the United States in the first half of the nineteenth century, relatively few European immigrants settled in the South. Why do you think most European immigrants settled permanently in the North rather than the South?

# A Letter to the Editor

Imagine that you are an **abolitionist** (antislavery activist) in the 1850s. Write a letter to the editor of your local newspaper arguing against slavery. Use one of the following statements as the main idea of your letter.

*Slavery directly contradicts the religious principles of this country.*

*Slavery directly contradicts the American principles of liberty and equality.*

*Slavery is a wedge that is going to divide the nation.*

**Slavery in the United States was abolished by the passage of the Thirteenth Amendment in 1865.**

# North and South

Dating back to the days of the American colonies, the North and the South were fundamentally different. The economy of the North was industrial, whereas the economy of the South was agricultural. These differences greatly contributed to the tensions that led to the Civil War. Do you think that today the North and the South are more similar than they are different? Explain.

© 2004 SparkNotes LLC

The Civil War took place between 1861 and 1865.

# Slave and Master

White plantation owners often responded to critics of slavery by claiming that the relationship between a slave master and a slave resembled the relationship between a father and a member of his family. Write a one-paragraph response to such a statement.

**Slavery was abolished in the United States in 1865.**

# An Interview with Mr. Douglass

Frederick Douglass was born a slave in Maryland around 1817. He escaped captivity and fled to the North, where he became the famous and influential spokesman of the African-American abolitionists, and a highly successful author and speaker. If you could interview Douglass, what would you ask him? Compile a list of ten questions.

Frederick Douglass died in 1895.

# Murderer or Martyr?

A passionate abolitionist named John Brown came up with an interesting scheme in 1857. His plan was to invade the South, liberate the slaves, and create a free state for the ex-slaves. In an attempt to provide slaves with weapons, he attacked an arsenal in Harpers Ferry, Virginia, and several innocent people lost their lives. Brown was tried for treason and murder, found guilty, and hanged. Was John Brown a murderer or a martyr? Explain your views.

**John Brown raided Harper's Ferry in 1859.**

# The Civil War Begins

After the election of 1860, in which Abraham Lincoln was elected president, South Carolina seceded from the Union. Ten other states followed its lead, forming the Confederate States of America. President Lincoln decided that he could not allow the country to break apart and that only military force could save the Union. The Civil War began. What other options did Lincoln have, if any, in his quest to save the nation?

The Civil War began officially in April 1861, when shots were fired at Fort Sumter.

# Our Side vs. Our Side

How did the size of the populations of the Union and the Confederacy compare to each other?

**The Confederate States of America were established in February 1861.**

# Pants and Shirts and Dresses

We now ask for large shirts, or pants in size six. But it was not always thus. What spurred the standardization of clothing sizes? If you're not sure, try to come up with a plausible explanation.

This standardization began during the Civil War.

# A Little Now, a Lot Later

The Homestead Act set aside millions of acres of land for settlers in the West. Settlers had two ways to get approximately 160 acres of land. They could either live on the land for five years and then pay about $30, or live on the land for six months and then pay $1.25 per acre. If you were a settler, which option would you choose? Why?

The Homestead Act was passed in 1862.

# I Am Going to Fight for the North

Imagine that you are a young man who has just volunteered to fight as a Union soldier in the Civil War. Write a letter to your parents explaining why you are going to fight.

**The Civil War took place between 1861 and 1865.**

# I Am Going to Fight for the South

Imagine that you are a young man who has just volunteered to fight as a Confederate soldier in the Civil War. Write a letter to your parents explaining why you are going to fight.

# March to the Sea

What did General Sherman's March entail? Why did it cause such lasting resentment?

General Sherman marched to the sea in the spring of 1864.

# The Little Lady

When Abraham Lincoln met Harriet Beecher Stowe, author of the novel *Uncle Tom's Cabin*, he reportedly said to her,

"So you're the little lady who made this big war."

Based on Lincoln's comments, what do you think Harriet Beecher Stowe's novel was about?

*Uncle Tom's Cabin* **was published in 1852.**

# Southern Independence

The American Revolution has been called the War for American Independence. The War of 1812 has been called the Second War for Independence. Could the Civil War be called the War for Southern Independence? Explain your answer.

The Civil War took was fought between 1861 and 1865.

# Four Score and Seven Years Ago

Read the first two sentences of Abraham Lincoln's famous Gettysburg Address and then summarize them in your own words.

"Four score and seven years ago our fathers brought forth on this continent a new nation, conceived in liberty and dedicated to the proposition that all men are created equal. Now we are engaged in a great civil war, testing whether that nation or any nation so conceived and so dedicated can long endure."

**President Lincoln delivered the Gettysburg Address in November 1863.**

# Teaching Freedmen

In 1865, Congress created the Freedmen's Bureau to educate, feed, and clothe former slaves and white refugees. If you were in charge of the education of the freedmen in 1865, what would you teach them so that they would be well-equipped to succeed in the post-slavery South? Explain your answer.

Slavery was abolished in the United States in 1865.

# Sticking it to the South

During the process of Reconstruction, many Northern politicians, including President Andrew Johnson, wanted to show no mercy toward the South. These men wanted to punish the South for seceding and for supporting slavery. If you were a Northern legislator, would you rule and rebuild the South with an iron fist, or would you show mercy? Explain your answer.

**Reconstruction took place between 1867 and 1877.**

# Scalawags and Carpetbaggers

During Reconstruction, the South was flooded with **scalawags** and **carpetbaggers**. Scalawags were Southerners who cooperated with the Reconstructionists, and carpetbaggers were "Yankees" who went south to make a profit from the rebuilding of the region. Why might Southerners have resented these groups?

© 2004 SparkNotes LLC

**Reconstruction took place between 1867 and 1877.**

# We'll Take Alaska

Secretary of State William H. Seward bought Alaska from Russia for the bargain-basement price of $7.2 million. Seward thought gold, furs, and other natural resources might be found in Alaska, but his fellow politicians scoffed at the purchase and called it **Seward's Folly**. Imagine you are Seward. Write a letter to your fellow Americans explaining why, in the midst of Reconstruction, you think it's a good idea to spend millions of dollars on frozen land that doesn't even border another state.

**Seward brokered the purchase of Alaska in 1867.**

# The President on Trial

President Andrew Johnson will go down in history as the first president to be **impeached** (accused of a crime while in office). Do you believe that a president should be exempt from being formally charged with a crime while in office? Should there be any exceptions? Explain your answers.

President Johnson, who served from 1865 to 1869, was impeached in 1868.

# Fined for Voting

In 1872, Susan B. Anthony broke the law by voting; at that time it was illegal for women to vote. For this crime she was tried, found guilty, and fined $100. Why do you think Anthony was willing to undergo such an ordeal just to vote? In her place, would you have done the same thing? Why or why not?

**Women were given the right to vote in 1920 with the passage of the Nineteenth Amendment.**

# Tycoon's Profits

Tycoon Andrew Carnegie, who made his fortune in steel, controlled every step on the way toward the final product. His miners mined the ore, his ships transported the ore, and his refineries fired and finished the ore. How do you think this process maximized profits for Carnegie?

Andrew Carnegie was born in 1835 and died in 1919.

# Pushing Pendleton

The Pendleton Act instituted civil service reform. Prior to the Pendleton Act, government jobs often went to campaign supporters or family members. How might civil service exams and merit-based promotions strengthen government?

The Pendelton Act was passed in 1883.

# Mudslinging

The presidential campaign that pitted Republican James Blaine against Democrat Grover Cleveland was perhaps the most vicious, mudslinging campaign in history. Mudslinging involves name-calling, insulting, and rumor-mongering during a campaign. Do you think this age-old practice is an effective method of campaigning? Is it an ethical method? Explain your answers.

**Blaine and Cleveland campaigned against each other in 1884.**

# Dirty Meat

During the Spanish-American War, American troops ate what they called "embalmed beef." How did the beef get this name? If you're not sure, come up with a plausible explanation.

The Spanish-American War was fought between February and December of 1898.

# Letter to the Farm

In the decades following the Civil War, many Americans moved from the countryside to cities. Imagine that you have just moved to a city and write a letter to the people back home about how your new life differs from life on the farm.

The Civil War was fought between 1861 and 1865.

# Typewriters and Telephones

The nineteenth century was an era of great inventions in the United States. Look at the list of inventions below and order them from most to least important (in your opinion). Then explain why you ranked the top three inventions as most important.

**1834**: Refrigerator invented by Jacob Perkins

**1837**: Morse code invented by Samuel Morse

**1853**: Elevator invented by Elisha Graves Otis

**1873**: Typewriter invented by Christopher Latham Sholes

**1876**: Telephone invented by Alexander Graham Bell

**1877**: Gramophone invented by Thomas Edison

**1879**: Light bulb invented by Thomas Edison

**1886**: Dishwasher invented by Josephine Cochran

# Zippers and Gum

Many people forget about the inventions of the nineteenth century that weren't quite as revolutionary as the telephone and the light bulb. Look at the list of fun inventions below and rank them from most to least necessary (in your opinion). Then explain why you ranked the top three inventions as most necessary.

**1851**: Ice cream invented by Jacob Fussell

**1863**: Roller skates invented by James Plimpton

**1870**: Chewing gum invented by Thomas Adams

**1884**: Fountain pen invented by L. E. Waterman

**1885**: Electric toothbrush invented by Dr. G. A. Scott

**1888**: Revolving door invented by Theophilu von Kannel

**1893**: Breakfast cereal invented by William Kellogg

**1893**: Zipper invented by Whitcomb Judson

# Ranking the Railroad

Some historians argue that the railroad was the greatest technological development in the United States in the nineteenth century. Write a paragraph or two agreeing or disagreeing with this position.

**The first railroad charter in America was granted in 1815.**

# Killing an Alligator

In 1865, the boiler of a boat exploded on the Mississippi River and 1,547 people died. But one man saved himself by killing an alligator trapped in a wooden crate, then clinging to the crate himself and getting to safety. Make up your own survival story, using this maritime disaster as inspiration.

© 2004 SparkNotes LLC

During the Civil War, the Mississippi River was a scene of frequent violence as both sides fought to control it. The Union won the struggle.

# Exploited Factory Workers

During the Industrial Revolution, many people found work in the new factories that had opened. Factory workers were often exploited, forced to work long hours for little money. Labor unions were the workers' only voice—their only bargaining tool with management. Why do you think labor unions were more effective than individuals in dealing with management and employers?

**The American Industrial Revolution took place between 1780 and 1860.**

# Resentful Americans

During the latter part of the nineteenth century, Americans known as **nativists** began to resent the foreign immigrants who were flooding the country. Some nativists even formed anti-foreigner organizations such as the American Protective Association (APA). Why do you think these nativists resented foreigners?

**The American Protective Association was founded in 1887 in Iowa.**

# A Nation of Readers

After the Civil War, newspaper and magazine circulation went through the roof, as did book sales. What do you think caused this phenomenon?

The Civil War ended in 1865.

# Stiffing the Confederates

The Pension Act of 1890 gave large pensions to all soldiers who fought for the Union during the Civil War, provided they fought for at least ninety days and were unable to work after the war. Do you think it's fair that the government didn't offer these pensions to former Confederate soldiers in the same situation? Why or why not?

The Pension Act, while popular, depleted the government's surplus at the time.

# On Strike in Chicago

The Pullman Palace Car Company, a railroad company, owned a town for rail employees outside Chicago. In 1894, the Pullman Company cut wages by about a third, but it kept rents in the town at the same level. The railroad workers went on strike, paralyzing rail traffic throughout Chicago. The military broke up the strike. Do you think the rail workers had a right to strike under these circumstances? Why or why not?

# Yellow Journalists

One of the factors contributing to the outbreak of the Spanish-American War was the sensational writing of **yellow journalists**. So-called yellow journalists exaggerated and embellished facts and appealed to readers' emotions in order to sway public opinion toward war. Do you think current journalism ever turns "yellow"? Explain, giving specific examples.

**The Spanish-American War lasted from February 1898 to December 1898.**

# White Man's Burden

Near the end of the nineteenth century, the United States took control of a number of territories, including Hawaii and Puerto Rico. The practice of adding territory in this way is known as **imperialism**. Some people believed that imperialism was the only option because of the **White Man's Burden**—the responsibility of nations like Britain and the U.S. to overtake and educate poorer, less "civilized" people. Do you think the White Man's Burden was a legitimate idea or just an excuse for imperialism? Explain your answer.

**Hawaii and Puerto Rico were annexed in July and December of 1898, respectively.**

# Across the Globe

During the late 1800s and early 1900s, many millions of people immigrated to the United States in search of a new life. These immigrants arrived from Italy, Germany, Ireland, England, China, and many other countries across the globe. Write a short explanation of how your own family came to the United States.

© 2004 SparkNotes LLC

Beginning in the 1840s, Europeans poured into America; between 1820 and 1980, some thirty-seven million Europeans moved to the United States.

# Melted or Tossed

Because of the large numbers of immigrants who have settled in the United States over the years, America has been called a **melting pot**. Some people dislike this term and say America is more like a **tossed salad** than a melting pot. What do you think the terms "melting pot" and "tossed salad" actually mean? Define both terms in your own words.

The term "melting pot" can be traced to a book J. Hector St. John Crevecoeur, *Letters from an American Farmer* (1782). In this book, Crevecoeur writes that in America, "all nations are melted into a new race of men."

# San Francisco Shaken

In 1906, a massive earthquake measuring around 8.3 on the Richter scale devastated San Francisco, killing over 500 people and decimating much of the city. Imagine you were in the city during the earthquake and write an account of what you saw and heard.

**Reconstruction took place between 1867 and 1877.**

# A Big Stick

It was Theodore "Teddy" Roosevelt who said of U.S. foreign policy, "Speak softly and carry a big stick." What did he mean by this?

**Theodore Roosevelt served as president from 1901 to 1909.**

# Kids at Work

During the early twentieth century, many children as young as five and six were working all day every day picking fruit, packing meat, selling papers, or doing some other form of physical labor. Child labor was one of the targets of activists known as **Progressives**.

Think like a Progressive and create a list of the top ten reasons why children shouldn't be forced to work. While you're compiling your list, consider the dangers that children face in the workplace and the opportunities they miss because of time spent at work.

**The time period from 1890 to 1913 is known as the Progressive Era.**

# Muckrakers

**Muckrakers** were reporters who, in the early 1900s, investigated social injustices and exposed them in print. Newspaper and magazine editors financed extensive research to guarantee the reliability of the muckrakers' reports. Imagine you are an editor. Why do you think spending money to ensure accuracy is worthwhile?

President Roosevelt coined the term "muckrake" in a 1906 speech.

# Meatpackers

One of the worst examples of corruption at the turn of the twentieth century was the meat packing and meat processing business. Dead rats, pieces of ropes, and other debris were often scooped up and deposited in potted ham or other processed meats.

Write a letter to the president of a meatpacking plant expressing your concern over such practices.

**Muckrakers scrutinized the meatpacking industry during the Progressive Era (1890–1913). Upton Sinclair exposed the meatpacking industry in his 1906 book *The Jungle*.**

# Teddy and the Forests

President Teddy Roosevelt pioneered legislation known as the Forest Reserve Act that set aside over 40 million acres of forest land for national parks and wildlife reserves. Do you believe this was a wise move? How might the landscape of the U.S. be different today if Roosevelt hadn't been so concerned about the environment? Explain.

**The Forest Reserves Act passed in 1891.**

# A Virtuous War

When President Woodrow Wilson reluctantly asked Congress to enter World War I against the Central Powers, he said that the United States should enter the war because "neutrality is no longer feasible or desirable where the peace of the world is involved" and "the world must be made safe for democracy." Do you think it's more virtuous to go to war for these reasons than it is to go to war to expand an empire or take revenge on an enemy? Explain your answers.

# Down on the League

In 1919, when the U.S., France, and Britain hammered out the Treaty of Paris that supposedly ended World War I, one of the provisions was the League of Nations—a beloved project of Woodrow Wilson's. It was decided that members of the league would be required to go to war against any nation that attacked another member nation. Congress refused to go along with such a plan. Why do you think Congress refused?

**The League of Nations, a precursor to the United Nations, was dissolved during World War II.**

# On the Mountain

Whose faces are carved on Mount Rushmore?

**Sculptor Gutzon Borglum spent fourteen years (1927–1941) carving Mount Rushmore.**

# No Drinks

The Eighteenth Amendment, ratified by the states in 1919, made alcohol illegal throughout the country. The Prohibition era changed the United States dramatically. (The Eighteenth amendment was later repealed by the Twenty-first Amendment in 1933.)

What do you think the United States would be like if a new Prohibition amendment passed this year? List a few of the major changes that you think would occur.

# Give Women the Vote

Before the ratification of the Nineteenth Amendment, American women were not allowed to vote. Put yourself in the position of a lobbyist working to convince legislators that women deserve **suffrage** (the right to vote). Compile a list of at least three reasons why women should be granted suffrage.

The Nineteenth Amendment was passed in 1920.

# Isolating America

After World War I, the United States hoped to limit or end American involvement in foreign affairs—a practice known as **isolationism**. Why do you think Americans were cautious about getting involved in foreign affairs after "The Great War"?

**The United States adhered to isolationist policies between 1921 and 1933.**

# Rich and Crazy

The 1920s (sometimes known as "The Roaring Twenties") was a time of baseball, jazz, dancing, daring stunts, outrageous fashions, and extravagant spending. It was also a time of relative economic prosperity for the United States. Do you think wild behavior usually goes along with riches? Back up your argument with a few examples, either of individuals, of nations, or of other periods in United States history.

**Reconstruction took place between 1867 and 1877.**

# Scopes on Trial

In 1925, a high school biology teacher from Tennessee named John Scopes was put on trial for teaching evolution to his students. Why do you think Scopes's behavior so shocked the residents of Tennessee? Can you imagine such a thing happening today in the United States? Explain.

The judge in the Scopes trial ruled that Darwin's theories were corrected, and the trial dealt with the sole question of whether Scopes taught evolution.

# At the Talkies

In the 1920s, mass entertainment started to emerge in the form of radio, movies with sound (called "talkies"), and sporting events like baseball. Imagine that after years of watching silent films, you see your first talkie. Write a paragraph-long letter to a friend describing the experience.

**"The Jazz Singer" (1927) was the first talkie in America.**

# Losing the Bank's Money

During the 1920s, many investors borrowed money from banks in order to speculate in the stock market. This practice was often a bad idea for the banks, the investors, and the companies who sold the stocks.

Come up with a scenario in which an investor could get in financial trouble after borrowing money from a bank and betting it on one stock.

**The United States stock market expanded quickly during the 1920s.**

# Dad Loses His Job

The Great Depression, which lasted from 1929 to 1939, devastated America. Up to thirty percent of working Americans lost their jobs; members of the middle class became homeless; children went hungry. Imagine you are a child in a middle-class family. Many of your friends' fathers have lost their jobs, and you have just found out that your father has lost his job. Write a brief journal entry describing your fears about the future.

The plight of Americans during the Great Depression was immortalized in John Steinbeck's novel *The Grapes of Wrath* (1939).

# Alphabet Soup

The administration of FDR was often referred to as the "Alphabet Soup Administration" because it created many new, acronym-friendly government offices and agencies, including the CCC (Civilian Conservation Corps), the WPA (Works Progress Administration) and the TVA (Tennessee Valley Authority). Make a list of six current government offices or agencies that add to the alphabet soup.

**President Roosevelt served from 1933 to 1945.**

# Third Term

With the United States on the brink of entering World War II, FDR decided to run for an unprecedented third presidential term. Make a list of reasons why this could have been a good idea, and a list of reasons why this could have been a bad idea.

President Roosevelt began his third term in 1941. The Twenty-second Amendment, passed in 1951, limited presidential terms to two.

# Believing the Reports

The American public did not truly take in the horror of Adolf Hitler's regime until years after the existence of concentration camps was first reported in American newspapers. Partly this was the fault of the media, which did not give prominent placement to news of the Holocaust. What other factors do you think contributed to the long delay in understanding the Holocaust?

The Holocaust took place between 1933 and 1945.

# Money for War

The war effort of World War II stimulated the United States economy and helped pull the nation out of the Great Depression. Why do you think the war had this effect? What sorts of industries benefit from a war?

**World War II was fought between 1935 and 1945. The Great Depression began in 1929.**

# Pearl Harbor and the World Trade Center

Many veterans of World War II have said that their emotions after the attacks of September 11, 2001, resembled their emotions after the Japanese attacked Pearl Harbor on December 7, 1941. Write a journal entry as if you are a student living in 1941 who has just heard the news of the Pearl Harbor attack.

**The surprise attack on Pearl Harbor led the United States to enter World War II.**

# WWII Posters

During wartime, the government often uses media to encourage people to participate in the war effort. During World War II, the government produced posters, most of which encouraged young men to enlist for active duty. Other posters urged women to work in factories or show support in other ways. Sketch two WWII posters, one meant for men and the other for women.

**World War II was fought between 1935 and 1945.**

# A Million Lives or the Bomb

The year is 1945 and the Japanese have not yet surrendered. You are President Harry Truman. Your advisors have informed you that forcing a Japanese surrender through continued conventional fighting may cost as many as one million American lives. You have another option: dropping the newly developed atomic bomb on Japan, thereby killing hundreds of thousands of Japanese. Which option do you choose? Why?

**Harry Truman was president from 1945 to 1953.**

# A Helping Hand for Europe

After World War II, the United States invested billions of dollars in the **Marshall Plan**, a scheme to rebuild Europe and give financial assistance to those European nations that sustained heavy damage during the war. Why do think American decision-makers believed that this was a good use of American funds?

The Marshall Plan, laid out in a speech by Secretary of State **George C. Marshall**, was adopted in 1944.

# Send the Troops to College

After U.S. servicemen returned from WWII, Congress passed the GI Bill of Rights, which offered many opportunities for the returned soldiers to continue or begin their educations. What short-term and long-term effects do you think the GI Bill of Rights had on the men and women who took advantage of the opportunities it offered?

**The GI Bill of Rights was adopted in 1944.**

# Winner, Then Loser

In 1948, on the night of the presidential election, the *Chicago Tribune* printed a front-page headline that read, "Dewey Defeats Truman." According to the article, Thomas Dewey had defeated Harry Truman and would be the next President of the United States. However, America awoke the next morning to learn that Truman was actually the winner.

Imagine that you are Thomas Dewey. Write a journal entry describing your feelings on election night after you learn that you have won the election. Write a second journal entry the following morning after you discover that Truman defeated you.

**In 1972, the Chicago Tribune gave a plaque to the Truman Library inscribed with a remembrance of the 1948 error.**

# Only Two

In reaction to FDR's unprecedented four terms as president, Congress passed the Twenty-second Amendment in 1951, limiting presidential tenure to two terms. Dwight Eisenhower objected to the amendment, saying,

"By and large, the United States ought to be able to choose for its President anybody that it wants, regardless of the number of terms he has served."

Do you agree with Eisenhower or do you believe that presidential tenure should be limited? Explain your answer.

The Twenty-second Amendment passed in 1951.

# Firing the General

In 1951, President Truman fired General Douglas Macarthur, who had publicly denigrated Truman for confining the Korean War to the Korean peninsula. Do you think officers deserve to be fired if they voice opinions that contradict those of their commander in chief? Why or why not?

**The Korean War was fought between 1950 and 1953.**

# Fighting a Cold War

In the decades following World War II, the United States and the Soviet Union fought the Cold War, which was a conflict of economics and politics, not really of weapons. How did these two superpowers wage this Cold War and what "weapons" did each side use? Who ultimately won the Cold War?

The Cold War is said to have begun in 1947, when Joseph Stalin refused to accept the Marshall Plan.

# Names of States

What is the most common first letter for state names?

# National Highways

Part of President Dwight Eisenhower's legacy is the vast interstate highway system. Eisenhower's highway construction project was initially valued at nearly $30 billion. What effects do you think this project had on trade and unemployment rates in the United States? Explain.

**Dwight D. Eisenhower was president from 1953 to 1961. Congress passed the Federal Aid Highway Act in 1956.**

# Segregation on the Basis of Race

In the Supreme Court case *Brown v. Topeka Board of Education*, the Supreme Court had to decide whether racial segregation of public schools was legal. The Court faced the question,

> "Does segregation of children in public schools solely on the basis of race, even though the physical facilities and other tangible factors may be equal, deprive the children of the minority group of equal educational opportunities?"

First, rewrite this question in your own words. Second, answer the question as if you were the Chief Justice of the Supreme Court. (Note that the Court ruled that segregation was indeed illegal.)

**The Supreme Court heard *Brown v. Topeka Board of Education* in 1954.**

# Red Scare

At the height of the Cold War, a paranoia known as the **Red Scare** swept across America. Many upstanding citizens across the country were accused of being Communists, or "reds," and were arrested and sometimes even brought before Congress for formal hearings. A government committee known as the House Un-American Activities Committee (HUAC) led the witch hunt. Former President Harry Truman said of HUAC,

> "I've said many times that the Un-American Activities Committee in the House of Representatives was the most un-American thing in America."

Why do you think Truman had such strong feelings toward this organization? Why might such an organization be dangerous?

**The HUAC, which was established in 1937, conducted a series of hearings in 1947 and 1948.**

# Racing for Space

During the Cold War, the Americans and Soviets engaged in a **Space Race**. Both were bent on conquering the "final frontier"—space. Dwight Eisenhower said,

"Will outer space be preserved for peaceful use and developed for the benefit of all mankind? Or will it become another focus for the arms race—and thus an area of dangerous and sterile competition?"

Why do you think the U.S. government considered winning the Space Race important? Make a list of reasons.

© 2004 SparkNotes LLC

The Space Race is said to have begun in 1960.

# Sweaty vs. Boyish

The presidential election of 1960 featured an unprecedented series of televised debates between Nixon and Kennedy. Many commentators noticed that Nixon appeared uneasy and sweaty on television, while Kennedy looked boyish and confident. Kennedy ultimately won the election. How did TV change the way presidential candidates campaigned? How did TV change public perceptions of candidates? Explain.

**John F. Kennedy was president from 1961 to 1963.**

# The Survival and the Success of Liberty

President John F. Kennedy once declared,

> "We shall pay any price, bear any burden, meet any hardship, support any friend, oppose any foe, to insure the survival and the success of liberty."

Do you believe the U.S. has a responsibility to follow this philosophy? What are some possible consequences of acting according to this philosophy? Explain your answers.

John F. Kennedy was president from 1961 to 1963.

# The Brink of Nuclear War

For fourteen days in 1962, the United States and the Soviet Union teetered on the brink of nuclear war. Soviet leader Khrushchev positioned Soviet missiles in Cuba, and U.S. President John F. Kennedy demanded that the Soviets withdraw them. Both sides seemed ready to start a nuclear war.

Imagine that you are either an American or a Russian student during the Cuban missile crisis. Write a diary entry about what you're feeling.

**Khrushchev acceded to the United States's demands, a capitulation that enraged Cuba's future leader, Fidel Castro.**

# Lunch Counter Protest

In 1960, a few black college students protested against segregated restaurants by staging a sit-in at a lunch counter in Greensboro, North Carolina. The nonviolent tactic proved effective.

What other nonviolent protest tactics can you think of? Which do you consider most useful? Which would you employ if you wanted to protest something? Explain your answers.

# A Tax on Voters

In the midst of the Civil Rights Movement of the 1960s, the nation ratified the Twenty-fourth Amendment, which outlawed a poll tax for federal elections. Whom do you think poll taxes were originally meant to affect, and how?

The Twenty-fourth Amendment was passed in 1964.

# Wallace for Segregation

In June of 1963, Alabama Governor George Wallace stood in the doorway of an Alabama university to physically prevent two African-American students from entering the school. The governor actually proclaimed, "Segregation now! Segregation tomorrow! Segregation forever!" Write a letter to Governor Wallace criticizing his position on segregation.

# Get Out the Vote

During the 1960s, civil rights activists traveled throughout the South to help minority citizens register to vote. President Lyndon Johnson aided the Civil Rights Movement by sending federal voting registrars to the South and by pushing through legislation that outlawed literacy tests for potential voters. Minority citizens already had the right to vote, so why do you think civil rights activists had to work so hard to get out the vote?

**Lyndon Johnson was President from 1963 to 1969.**

# The True Meaning of its Creed

"I have a dream that one day this nation will rise up and live out the true meaning of its creed: 'We hold these truths to be self-evident, that all men are created equal.'"

Martin Luther King, Jr., spoke these words during the Civil Rights Movement. What do you think Dr. King meant by these words? Do you think his dream has been accomplished in the United States?

**Dr. King delivered his "I Have a Dream" speech in Washington, D.C., on August 28, 1963.**

# Ignoring a Murder

In 1964, a woman named Kitty Genovese was stabbed to death in a courtyard in Queens, New York. Although many of her neighbors heard her crying out for help and some even looked down at the scene from their windows, no one intervened or called the cops. What do you think might have caused her neighbors to act as they did?

# Against Poverty

President Lyndon B. Johnson launched what he called the **War on Poverty**. If you were in charge of a war on poverty, what would you do? What measures would you take to combat poverty?

**Lyndon B. Johnson was President from 1964 to 1968.**

# Miranda Rights

In 1963, a man named Ernesto Miranda was arrested. Upon his arrest, he confessed to the crime of which he was accused. Miranda later said that he wouldn't have confessed if he had known that confessions weren't mandatory and that his confession would be used against him. The Supreme Court, in *Miranda v. Arizona* (1966), said that a suspect must be told that he has the right to remain silent, that anything he says can and will be used against him in court, and that he has the right to an attorney. These are now known as **Miranda warnings**. Why do you think the Supreme Court would go so far to protect the rights of someone accused of a crime?

U.S. HISTORY

# Women to Work

During World War II, women worked in factories and at other jobs. After the war ended, they demanded more opportunities in all walks of life. During the 1950s and 1960s, women went to work in increasing numbers, earning more pay and breaking into fields that had been dominated by men. Make a list of jobs that were essentially off-limits to women prior to the 1950s and 1960s.

# Hippie Culture

During the 1960s, a counterculture emerged in the United States unlike any the country had seen before. Hippies and students across the country questioned authority, pushed social boundaries, and explored new religions and philosophies. These new attitudes were reflected in the music, art, and fashion of the era. Have you observed any similar (if less powerful) counterculture groups or movements in your lifetime? If so, describe them.

# Army Yes, Vote No

Prior to the Twenty-sixth Amendment, which was ratified in 1971, eighteen-year-olds were eligible to be drafted into the military but weren't allowed to vote. Imagine that you are an eighteen-year-old living in 1969. Write a letter to your congressman expressing your feelings about this contradiction.

# Voter Apathy

George Jean Nathan observed,

"Bad officials are elected by good citizens who do not vote."

What did he mean by this? Why do you think many Americans don't vote?

George Jean Nathan was born in 1882 and died in 1958.

# Executive Privilege

In 1972, President Richard Nixon was named as a co-conspirator in the Watergate scandal, a scandal in which high-level members of the Republican Party broke into the Democratic National Committee's headquarters with Nixon's knowledge. When Nixon's files, including tape-recorded conversations that took place in the Oval Office, were subpoenaed, Nixon cited **executive privilege** and refused to hand them over. The case went all the way to the Supreme Court, which decided that executive privilege applies only if the president is protecting military, diplomatic, or national security secrets.

Do you think a president should be exempt from handing over "confidential" information even when subpoenaed? If so, why and in what situations? If not, why not?

© 2004 SparkNotes LLC

**Richard Nixon was President from 1969 until his resignation in August 1974.**

# Tet Effect

The **Tet Offensive** was one of the turning points of the Vietnam War, in which the United States supported South Vietnam. During the Tet Offensive, North Vietnamese forces attacked South Vietnamese cities. North Vietnam didn't take any cities and lost many of its soldiers. Still, many people argued that it "won" the battle. How is this possible?

**The Tet Offensive occurred in 1968.**

# The War on TV

The Vietnam conflict was the first major military conflict to be televised. Footage of the war appeared each night on the news. How do you think this TV coverage affected the way Americans perceived war in general and Vietnam in particular?

American involvement in Vietnam began in the 1950s and ended in 1973.

# Roe v. Wade

In 1973, the Supreme Court heard *Roe v. Wade*. The justices determined that a woman's right to privacy, including her right to terminate her pregnancy, outweighs the state's right to intervene to preserve the health of either the woman or the unborn child. The Court also said, though, that the state's right increases as the pregnancy progresses. Explain your own beliefs about abortion.

# 55 Miles per Hour

In 1973, Arab oil-producing countries put an embargo on oil to the United States —that is, they refused to sell oil to the U.S. As a result, the U.S. faced a severe oil shortage and an energy crisis. Congress responded with a number of measures, including imposing a nationwide speed limit of 55 mph to conserve fuel. If the U.S. faced such an energy crisis today, what measures could the country impose in order to conserve energy?

# Unelected VP

Not long after Vice President Spiro T. Agnew resigned from office because of the Watergate scandal, Congress selected Gerald Ford to be the new vice president. When Nixon resigned his office as president, Ford became President of the United States. He was the first president in U.S. history to gain presidential office without being elected either vice president or president.

Should there be a safeguard that prohibits a person from ascending to the highest office in the land in such a manner? If so, what alternative would you propose? Explain your answer.

**Gerald Ford was appointed Vice President in 1973. He served as President from 1974 to 1977.**

# Canal Concerns

During the administration of President Jimmy Carter, the United States negotiated a treaty that required relinquishing control of the Panama Canal by the year 2000. Many Americans were upset about this, because Teddy Roosevelt had spent millions of dollars to dig the canal. Carter argued that U.S.–Latin American relations would benefit from the treaty.

If you were an advisor to Carter, would you have advised him to keep control of the canal or to give it up? Explain your reasoning.

**Jimmy Carter served as President from 1977 to 1981.**

# Running for President

Who was the first black person to make a serious bid for the presidency? When did he run?

# Problem Government

President Ronald Reagan once remarked,

> "Government is not the solution to our problem. Government is the problem."

What do you think Reagan meant by this statement? What are your own thoughts on the matter?

**Ronald Reagan was President from 1981 to 1989.**

# Money, Money, Money

During the Reagan administration, the United States spent record amounts on defense and the military. The intention was for America to head off aggressive action from its enemies, specifically the Soviets, by creating a larger, more powerful army. This practice paid off but left the nation with enormous debt. Do you think the result of the policy was worth the financial price that the country paid and is still paying? Explain your answer.

**Ronald Reagan was President from 1981 to 1989.**

# Hostage Disaster

In 1979, a group of Americans was taken hostage in Teheran. In 1980, American commandos went in to save them. Disaster ensued. Helicopters malfunctioned, eight soldiers died, and none of the hostages was freed at the time. If you were the President of the United States, would you authorize the rescue of hostages even if you knew there was great risk involved? Explain your answer.

# Supreme Court Woman

In 1981, Sandra Day O'Connor became the first woman to sit on the U.S. Supreme Court. Why do you think it took so long for a woman to be named to the Supreme Court? Why do you think Ronald Reagan, the most conservative president in fifty years, was the president who finally appointed a woman to the Court? Explain your answers.

# Delayed Payment

The Twenty-seventh Amendment, the most recent amendment to the U.S. Constitution, prohibits a raise for legislators from going into effect until after the following election. What do you think the nation hoped to prevent by ratifying this amendment?

**The Twenty-seventh Amendment was passed in 1992.**

# Combat Deaths

During the Gulf War, the United States lost 148 soldiers during combat. How many Iraqis died in combat, according to an estimate made by Saudi Arabia? If you're not sure, make an educated guess.

**The Gulf War began in January 1991 and ended in February 1991.**

# Lost the Battle, Won the War

The presidential election of 2000 was perhaps the wildest in U.S. history. Although Al Gore received slightly more popular votes than George Bush did, Bush won the election because he garnered more electoral votes, or votes in the Electoral College. This was not the first time the candidate with the most popular votes actually lost the election. Do you think it is fair for a candidate with fewer popular votes to win a presidential election? Why or why not?

In 1824, Andrew Jackson won the popular vote but lost to John Quincy Adams; in 1876, Samuel Tildon won the popular vote but lost to Rutherford Hayes; and in 1888, Grover Cleveland won the popular vote but lost to Benjamin Harrison.

# President and Soldier

No fewer than twenty-five of the men elected President of the United States served in the military before they were elected. In what ways could a president draw on his military experience while in office? Should there be a law requiring presidential candidates to have military experience? Explain your answers.

# 9/11

On September 11, 2001, the United States endured a deadly terrorist attack. How do you think the nation has changed since that time? What changes have you observed in your own town or city? Explain your answers.

# A New Anthem

After witnessing the bombing of Fort McHenry in 1814, Francis Scott Key wrote "The Star Spangled Banner," which was adopted as the American national anthem in 1931. Imagine that Congress has given you the task of creating a new national anthem, set to any tune you choose. Write the words for the new national anthem and note which tune you'd like to accompany your anthem.

**Francis Scott Key was born in 1779 and died in 1843.**

# Fruited Plains

Many people know the first stanza of "America the Beautiful" ("O beautiful for spacious skies," etc.), but the other three stanzas of the song are often neglected. Each stanza begins with the phrase "O beautiful for . . . ." What three other beautiful things, in addition to spacious skies, does the song mention?

Katherine Lee Bates wrote "America the Beautiful" in 1893. She amended it in 1904.

# "I Pledge Allegiance"

In 1892, Francis Bellamy published the pledge that has become a school staple:

> "I pledge allegiance to my Flag and the Republic for which it stands, one nation indivisible, with Liberty and Justice for all."

Congress changed these words slightly in 1954. What is the current text of the pledge?

**Francis Bellamy was born in 1855 and died in 1931.**

# Answers

1. Answers will vary.

2. Explorers wanted to spread religion, to discover riches, and to become famous and powerful.

3. Answers should include information about Africa, the Americas, Europe, slaves, and material goods.

4. Letters should include information about the scarcity of food, **conflicts** with Native Americans, and disease.

5. He was an American Indian from Pawtuxet (now Plymouth Bay) who spoke English; he is remembered for his friendship with American settlers in the 1620s.

6. Answers will vary.

7. From experience, the founders understood that a heterogeneous religious community (that is, a single community where multiple faiths are practiced) fostered conflicts. They probably wanted to avoid that strife.

8. Answers will vary.

9. Answers will vary. Students may suggest that older members of the clergy, used to presiding over traditional churches and congregations, may have objected to drastic change of any kind.

10. Answers will vary.

11. Answers should indicate that Britain was a guaranteed market for colonial goods. Answers to the second part of the question will vary.

12. Answers will vary.

13. Answers will vary.

14. Answers will vary.

15. The shots fired at Lexington set into motion a series of events that changed the course of history. Among other things, the fight showed

the world that the British conflict with the colonies was a serious one.

16. Answers will vary.

17. Answers will vary.

18. Answers will vary. Students may say that remaining loyal to Britain would ensure Britain's protection; would not incur loss of life, which would occur in a war for independence; and would avoid the reduction of freedoms that a loss to Britain would inevitably produce. On the other hand, students may say that declaring independence was the only logical response to Britain's offensive behavior.

19. Countries would tend to assume that the new nation would have financial problems, would return to Britain's protection, or would be conquered by another nation, among other possibilities.

20. A written constitution is much harder to misinterpret than an oral one.

21. A strong central government would provide cohesion for the newly-united colonies.

22. The founders hoped that a weak central government would decrease the likelihood that a tyrannical government would develop.

23. The farmers didn't want to pay taxes on whiskey. President George Washington stopped the rebellion by sending in 13,000 militiamen.

24. Answers will vary; translations may resemble the following: "Avoiding fights wasn't the purpose of creating three different branches of government. In fact, the founding fathers wanted to encourage fighting, which they thought would save the country from being taken over by a single person."

25. Answers will vary.

26. Answers will vary but may resemble the following: We the citizens of the United States, in order to create a better country, create fair laws, make sure we're a peaceful nation, keep the citizens safe, help the people to be prosperous and healthy, ensure we have the blessings of freedom for ourselves and our

children, create this Constitution for the United States of America.

27. Citizens of larger states liked the idea; citizens of smaller states with smaller debts felt cheated when the government assumed the larger debts of large states.

28. Answers will vary.

29. Students might mention newspapers, TV, and conversations.

30. Answers will vary.

31. The accused might wait indefinitely in jail without the right to a speedy trial. He might not be able to defend himself against accusations if he couldn't call his own witnesses.

32. The vice president serves as president of the Senate, casting the tie-breaking vote there when occasion warrants it. Also, he steps in for the president if the president cannot serve.

33. Answers will vary.

34. The large states liked their representation in the House, and the small states liked their representation in the Senate.

35. Answers will vary.

36. Answers will vary but might point out that term limits can have two opposing effects: they can either reduce the risk of abuse of office or they can result in the removal of an excellent public servant.

37. The cotton gin enabled faster, cheaper production of cotton; as a result, the price of cotton fell, more people bought it and used to make products of their own, and demand increased.

38. Answers will vary.

39. Answers will vary, but students will likely argue that the Sedition Act contradicts our constitutional rights to freedom of speech and freedom of the press.

40. This ability ensures that Congress cannot enact unjust laws.

41. By "entangling alliances," Jefferson meant binding obligations or secret alliances. Answers to the second part of the question will vary.

42. Answers will vary.

43. Answers will vary.

44. Mexico City, which was occupied in 1847, during the Mexican War (1846–1848).

45. Answers will vary, but students should include something like, "We're now an independent nation capable of defending ourselves."

46. Answers will vary.

47. Answers will vary.

48. Neither side wanted the other side to get the upper hand; an equal number of states per side ensured an impasse.

49. Answers will vary.

50. The pioneer mentality and rough-and-rugged lifestyle of the typical Southerner and Westerner made Jackson an appealing choice. The more cosmopolitan Northerner probably disliked Jackson's persona.

51. Answers will vary.

52. Answers will vary.

53. Answers will vary.

54. Answers will vary but may mention the division of students into grades, the use of modern technology, the subjects studied, and so on.

55. In 1835, Richard Lawrence, a house painter, attempted to kill Andrew Jackson. He had brought two pistols for the purpose, but both misfired.

56. Answers will vary.

57. Answers will vary.

58. Answers will vary.

59. Britain may have been interested in undermining the success of the U.S.; a new nation on America's doorstep would probably increase conflict.

60. Answers will vary.

61. Answers will vary.

62. Answers will vary.

63. Answers will vary.

64. The new new road improved the efficiency of travel, which led to more travelers, increased trade, and speedier trade.

65. Answers will vary.

66. The Know-Nothings were a violent group opposed to Catholics and foreigners. Under questioning, members of the group would say, "I know nothing," which is how they got their name.

67. Answers should indicate that the steamboat made all of these things considerably faster and more efficient.

68. Answers may mention the fact that river transportation was restricted to rivers, while railroads could be laid in any direction and could travel across rivers and mountains.

69. Answers will vary but should probably mention that the better-known presidents governed during important historical events.

70. More slaves might have tried to escape to free territory.

71. Most of the major seaports were in the North, as were factory jobs in cities.

72. Answers will vary.

73. Answers will vary.

74. Answers will vary.

75. Answers will vary.

76. Answers will vary.

77. Answers will vary.

78. The Union, with a population of around 20.7 million, outnumbered the Confederacy, with a population of around 9.1 million.

79. The Civil War. The Union, which needed to produce many, many uniforms, measured the bodies of over a million soldiers. These statistics eventually led to standardized clothing sizes.

80. Answers will vary.

81. Answers will vary but may mention the preservation of the Union, the liberation of the slaves, a sense of duty to one's country, or even a dislike of Southerners.

82. Answers will vary but may mention defense of a way of life, defense of the honor of the South, a response to Northern aggression, a sense of duty to the Confederacy, or even a dislike of Northerners.

83. Sherman's march across Georgia originated in Atlanta in 1864 and ended in Savannah. The march devastated Georgia; Sherman and his men burned buildings, looted, and generally wreaked havoc.

84. Answers will vary, but students will likely guess that the novel was about slavery.

85. Answers will vary.

86. Students may write something like, "Forty-seven years ago, our forefathers created a new nation. They created it with the idea of freedom in mind, and they dedicated it to the idea that all humans are born equal. Now we're in the midst of a civil war that is testing this idea that a nation dedicated to freedom and equality can survive."

87. Answers will vary but should mention reading, writing, and vocational skills.

88. Answers will vary.

89. Southerners were already resentful of the harsh Reconstruction conditions, and these two groups were seen as scavengers who sought to take advantage of people who were enduring difficult times.

90. Answers will vary.

91. Answers will vary.

92. Answers will vary.

93. Carnegie didn't have to pay anyone else for services rendered and he didn't have to spend any money outside his own company.

94. By rooting out nepotism and bringing the best qualified people, rather than the best connected people, into government.

95. Answers will vary.

96. The beef caused food poisoning and dysentery, among other diseases, thereby

killing many of the soldiers and leading to their burial, or "embalmment."

97. Answers should discuss the increased number of jobs in cities that new factories provided. Answers should also explain that city life was more crowded, less sanitary, and characterized by hustle and bustle.

98. Answers will vary.

99. Answers will vary.

100. Answers will vary.

101. Answers will vary.

102. Answers will vary but should probably suggest that individuals pose little threat, because they can be ignored or fired, whereas unions pose a genuine threat to employers.

103. Answers will vary but should mention the nativists' ignorance and their fear that the foreigners would take jobs away from native-born Americans.

104. Answers will vary but should point to the increased number of public schools and the subsequent increase in literacy.

105. Answers will vary; students may note that the Confederate soldiers were not employed by the U.S. government and, therefore, were not necessarily eligible for pensions from the U.S. government.

106. Answers will vary.

107. Answers will vary.

108. Answers will vary.

109. Answers will vary.

110. "Melting pot" suggests the blending of cultures, while "tossed salad" suggests the existence of cultures side by side.

111. Answers will vary.

112. Students should say something like, "Peaceful diplomacy should be accompanied by the presence of military might."

113. Answers will vary but should mention lack of safety and educational opportunity, exploitation of minors, and so on.

114. Answers will vary but should include a discussion of ethics and possible legal ramifications.

115. Answers will vary.

116. Answers will vary; students may mention that much of today's protected wilderness might otherwise have been mined, converted for agricultural use, or urbanized.

117. Answers will vary.

118. Answers should mention the fact that Congress wanted control over the decision to go to war.

119. George Washington, Thomas Jefferson, Abraham Lincoln, and Theodore Roosevelt.

120. Answers will vary.

121. Students might mention such justifications as the mandates of the Constitution, which guarantees representation to all citizens, and women's mental and moral equality with men.

122. Answers will vary but might point out that the American people were physically and emotionally exhausted from the war. Tired of the death and destruction, they did not want to endure such a struggle again.

123. Answers will vary.

124. Answers will vary.

125. Answers will vary.

126. Students should imagine a scenario in which the investment failed, leaving no money with which to repay the loan.

127. Answers will vary.

128. Answers may include such agencies as the FBI, CIA, FCC, SEC, and EPA.

129. Students may argue that the country needed continuity and that retaining a strong leader is more important than enforcing term limits; on the other side of the issue, they may argue that making exceptions for one president might lead to abuses in the future.

130. Answers may mention the difficulty of comprehending such a monstrous event, the power of denial, and prejudice against Jews.

131. Students should address the increase in production, the need for more workers, the opening of additional factories, and so on. Many industries benefited from the

war, including the munitions, aviation, and automobile industries.

132. Answers will vary.

133. Sketches will vary.

134. Answers will vary. Students should weigh the cost of lives, civilian casualties vs. military losses, the precedent set by the choice made, and the long-term consequences of using nuclear weapons.

135. Answers should mention the desire to prevent communist countries from rebuilding Europe.

136. Students should mention a better literacy rate, an increase in skilled workers, better-educated children, and so on.

137. Answers will vary.

138. Answers will vary.

139. Answers will vary.

140. Students should mention propaganda, spies, embargoes, and alliances. They should indicate that the West won the Cold War.

141. M and N are tied: M-states are: Maine, Maryland, Massachusetts, Michigan, Minnesota, Mississippi, Missouri, and Montana. N-states are: Nebraska, Nevada, New Hampshire, New Jersey, New Mexico, New York, North Carolina, and North Dakota.

142. Unemployment decreased and the efficiency, and therefore the profitability, of trade increased.

143. The rewritten question will resemble something like, "If black and white schools are equally well off, is segregation still bad for black students?" Answers to the second part of the question will vary.

144. Answers should point out the fact that HUAC's activities threatened people's Constitutional rights. Students might draw parallels to the old Alien Laws and the Sedition Act.

145. Answers will vary but might include the world's respect, gains in science, and historical importance.

146. Television made appearance and demeanor much more important, and the public probably started thinking less about candidates' positions and more about their deportment.

147. Answers will vary but might include the possibility of entangling alliances, the constant specter of war, and the possibility of spreading oneself thin.

148. Answers will vary.

149. Answers will vary.

150. Poll taxes were a tool used to discourage black people and the poor from voting.

151. Answers will vary.

152. Even though minorities technically had the right to vote, obstacles such as literacy tests, poll taxes, and harassment prevented or intimidated people from voting.

153. Answers will vary.

154. Answers will vary, but may mention fear of getting injured, numbness due to frequent exposure to crime, and the assumption that someone else would take care of the problem.

155. Answers will vary but may broach such issues as public education, voter registration, vocational training, financial assistance, and progressive taxation.

156. Stringent precautions taken during an arrest make it less likely that an innocent person will be convicted.

157. Answers may mention management, law, medicine, politics, and science, among other fields.

158. Answers might mention punk rock, grunge, the Goth movement, and so on.

159. Answers will vary.

160. Citizens affect elections even if they don't vote; sometimes they affect them by, for example, staying home and not voting for the

better-qualified candidate. In answer to the second part of the questions, students may cite voters' sense that there isn't a great deal of difference between the candidates or that the candidates can't make a difference anyway; ignorance about the issues and candidates or indifference to the issues and candidates; and dislike of politics.

161. Answers will vary.

162. The Tet Offensive weakened the support of the American people for the war in Vietnam, so in that sense North Vietnam succeeded.

163. For the first time, people saw gruesome, up-to-the-minute footage of war. It may have made the reality of war more vivid for people, and it likely made some people rethink the wisdom of fighting in Vietnam.

164. Answers will vary.

165. We could turn to solar power, electricity, hybrid engines, and gas rationing, among other options.

166. Answers will vary.

167. Answers will vary.

168. Jesse Jackson was the first black person to run for president. He ran twice, once in 1984 and once in 1988.

169. Students may point to the intrusiveness and size of government, or they may dismiss Reagan's remark as red meat for the Republican base. Answers to the second part of the question will vary.

170. Answers will vary.

171. Answers will vary.

172. Answers will vary.

173. People likely hoped to prevent politicians from giving themselves immediate, hefty raises.

174. 80,000–10,000 Iraqis died in combat, according to this estimate.

175. Answers will vary.

176. Answers will vary.

177. Answers will vary.

178. Answers will vary.

179. Pilgrim feet, heroes proved, and patriot dream.

180. "I pledge allegiance to the flag of the United States of America and to the Republic for which it stands, one nation under God, indivisible, with liberty and justice for all.